Mojola Akinyemi

Cara and Kelly are Best Friends Forever For Life

Salamander Street

PLAYS

First published in 2025 by Salamander Street Ltd., a Wordville imprint. (info@salamanderstreetcom).

Cara and Kelly are Best Friends Forever For Life, © Mojola Akinyemi, 2025

Cover Photography: Ché Deedigan
Cover Design: Kate Weir

PB ISBN: 9781068233418

10 9 8 7 6 5 4 3 2 1

Further copies of this publication can be purchased from
www.salamanderstreet.com

Wordville

INTRODUCTION

Mojola Akinyemi is a playwright, screenwriter and director born in Nigeria, and based in London and the South East of England. She studied English at the University of Cambridge, where she also wrote her debut play *Great Mother*. This was longlisted for the Mustapha Matura Award in 2021, the Bruntwood Playwriting competition in 2022 and the Women's Playwriting Award in 2023. Her second play *Imaginary Natural Beings* was staged at VAULT Festival 2023 and Theatro Technis during Camden Fringe 2023.

Cara and Kelly are Best Friends Forever For Life was initially staged for a readthrough performance at the Omnibus Theatre as part of their Next Page Season for January 2025, and has been developed across several months ahead of its performances at the Pleasance Courtyard (Bunker 3) during the Edinburgh Fringe Festival across July and August 2025.

ACKNOWLEDGEMENTS

I would like to express my endless gratitude for Hannah Samuel-Ogbu, my producer, confidant and incredible friend. Thank you for being the first person to hear about this play, and being there for me throughout the entire process, from writing it, to applying for a Fringe venue, to the redrafting process, to fundraising, to production, and every single stage in-between and outside of that. I simply could not have done this without you, and I will be forever grateful. 'Thank you' is simply not enough.

I must also say thank you to my director, Ilona Sell. Before I asked you to direct this play, you already provided extremely lucid and insightful comments, providing perspectives I wouldn't even think to consider, and helping me discover unexpected details in my writing. Your directing has been equally brilliant, if not more, and it has been a pleasure to build this play with you.

Thank you to my actors, Scarlett Stitt and Isobel Thom, for bringing Cara and Kelly to life. I approached Scarlett before the play had even been written, and she was one of the first people to read it, knowing instantly she wanted to play Cara. She sent the play to Isobel, who read it and understood Kelly on such a level that I knew instantly they were perfect for the part. It has been a great joy seeing you take these teenagers and make them your own, understanding the challenges that come with such difficult characters, but always approaching it with care, sensitivity and virtuosity.

Thank you to Jade Franks for your wonderful feedback on the first draft, and for helping me look at the play differently post-readthrough. Whilst I am writing this before we go up to Edinburgh, I already know I will have more thanks to you for the support you will provide throughout the month.

Thank you Alessandro Babalola, for taking the time to dissect this play with me. There's a certain point when you get so many notes that it can become overwhelming, but you helped me filter these and pick out what was useful, and highlight what I was actually trying to achieve with the play.

Thank you to my dramaturg Haiqing Liang. Your notes and comments in the breaking down of this play were so useful for the redraft, and the precision helped me draw out the core of the play and refine it.

Thank you to Pleasance, for believing in this play enough to stage it for the entire month. Pleasance was our dream venue and it is such an honour to be part of the 2025 season. And thank you to Liv and everyone at Chloe Nelkin Consulting for helping us get this play in the news, on the socials and in the front of people's minds. Thank you to the Omnibus Theatre, for the essential January readthrough and the London preview (along with the Seven Dials Playhouse). And thank you to Keep it Fringe, as well as our generous donors, for the funds that have boosted us on our path to Edinburgh.

Thank you to Ché Deedigan, for the fantastic image on the cover of this book, and for the phenomenal images from all our promo shoots. And thank you to Kate Weir, for the striking cover and poster design.

Thank you to Jethro Thompson, my agent at Curtis Brown, for championing this play, and for his continuous support with my writing career. And thank you to Salamander Street, for seeing something in this play and immortalising these words in print.

Thank you to my sister, Mope Akinyemi. I have so many thanks to give you, about this play and beyond that. Thank you for making me realise the gravity of what I was writing, and the responsibility I had to the topic and themes of the work. Thank you for the support you have given me over the years, always being ready to listen to an extract or a rant, and coming to every performance of everything. And thank you to the rest of my family, Mum, Dad and Mofi. Being a writer can be tricky and at times lonely, but the continuous support you have shown me is what allows me to carry on.

Thank you to everyone who has supported me in any way throughout this process. I can't name everyone, but I hold you all in my heart. And a final thank you for those who have watched (or read) this play. Theatre needs an audience, and I am so grateful to everyone who has been a part of it.

Mojola Akinyemi

Previews of *Cara and Kelly are Best Friends Forever For Life* were held in London at the Seven Dials Playhouse on the 23rd of July at 8:30pm, and Omnibus Theatre on the 26th of July at 8:30pm.

Performances at the Pleasance Courtyard, Bunker 3, ran from the 30th of July–25th of August (not 18th) at 3:20pm (preview performances on the 30th and 31st of July).

Cara:	**Scarlett Stitt**
Kelly:	**Isobel Thom**

Director:	**Ilona Sell**
Producer:	**Hannah Samuel-Ogbu**
Dramaturg & Assistant Director:	**Haiqing Liang**
Lighting Designer & Technician:	**Hugh Bowers**
Sound Designer:	**Liam Bratchford**
Cover Photography:	**Ché Deedigan**
Cover Design:	**Kate Weir**

THE CAST

Scarlett Stitt | Cara

Scarlett Stitt is an actor and artist based in London. Scarlett has been acting since the age of 11, after starring as Moody Margaret in Vertigo films *Horrid Henry* featuring Anjelica Houston and Richard E. Grant. She was a member of the Young Actor's Theatre from an early age, acting in film, television and theatre productions. She trained with Young Pleasance, National Youth Theatre, Lecoq and finally RADA. She now works professionally as an adult actor. Scarlett also makes her own work, and has just written her first full length play with the support of Soho theatre, previously winning an Offie Commendation and Audience Choice Award for her show *Kissing A Fool*. She runs a drag collective called Haus of Intrusive Thots and is a graduate of the Soho Theatre Drag & Cabaret Lab. She is a recipient of the Jack Petchey Award for outstanding young achiever.

Isobel Thom | Kelly

Isobel Thom trained at RWCMD and LAMDA. Their theatre credits include *I, Joan* and *A Midsummer Night's Dream* at Shakespeare's Globe. They won The Stage Debut Award for Best Performer in a Play (for *I, Joan*), were nominated for Actor of the Year 2023 (DIVA) and featured on the DIVA Power List 2023. Television includes *Big Mood* (Channel 4); *Too Much* (Netflix). Short film credits include *Waiting* (Accidental Donkey). Work whilst training includes *Moon Licks, Grimm Tales, Appropriate* and *After Miss Julie* at RWCMD; *King Lear* at LAMDA; *Adelante* for The Play List at the Royal Court.

Mojola Akinyemi

Cara and Kelly are Best Friends Forever For Life

CHARACTERS

CARA (C)
14 years old, white

KELLY (C)
13 then 14 years old, white

LOCATION

UK 2013

NOTES ON PRODUCTION

The play takes place across approximately six months (except for the final scene).

For the asterix (*) on page 19, the prison is said to be 'Belmarsh', but this should correlate with the closest prison geographically to wherever the play is being staged, and so can change when needed.

A forward slash (/) indicates overlapping dialogue.

An ellipsis (...) indicates a point where dialogue could be spoken, but the character is purposefully remaining silent. It is important for the actor to play this silence with as much emphasis as a spoken line.

I.

Lunchtime.

School corridor.

C: No.

K: Yeah!

C: Fuck off.

K: I'm serious.

C: She told you that?

K: No, Emily told me in the lunch queue, and *she* heard it from Tyla, and *she* saw both of them coming out of the disabled toilets.

C: I swear you can't even get in those without a key from the teachers.

K: Not the ones in the Witley Building. They've unlocked them.

C: Do you think they actually fucked?

K: No.

C: I do.

K: She's a slag, yeah, but she wouldn't have.

C: How do you know?

K: She told me. She's scared of doing it. She's got, like, a phobia of penis.

C: You're fucking joking.

K: No, so now Nathan's like, really good at fingering.

KELLY gestures.

K: He's like... a super fingerer.

C: Fucking hell.

K: I know.

C: She's still a slag.

K: I know / I said.

C: And now everyone's gonna know.

K: She's meant to be going for netball captain next year as well.

C: Yeah, but you were always gonna get that.

K: Well, yeah, I'd should do now. Not that it matters anyway, it's like, / whatever.

C: Don't pretend you don't care.

CARA opens a compact mirror.

K: No obviously yeah, but still.

C: My eyebrows look so clapped.

K: No they don't. You look fit.

C: I spent an hour doing them this morning. And they still look like shit.

K: Maybe you should get them tattooed.

C: I might.

KELLY leans to inspect CARA's face.

K: Holly's sister is training on doing those tattoos on her Health and Beauty course. She might do them for cheap.

C: You have to be 18.

K: She did them for Holly.

C: Holly's sister is a doughnut then. Her eyebrows look like sperm.

CARA snaps her compact mirror shut. She gets out a stick of gum. She places a stick in her mouth.

KELLY opens her mouth.

CARA places a stick of gum KELLY's mouth.

K: You ready for the match tonight?

C: Nah.

K: What?

C: Can't.

K: Why not?

C: Can't be bothered.

K: You've got to.

C: Haven't brung my PE kit.

K: What are you on about?

C: I forgot it.

K: So what, you're not gonna play in the match then?

C: Well, I can't can I? I haven't got my PE kit.

K: Can't you just borrow it from someone else?

C: No.

K: You can ask Alice.

C: Eurgh, no thanks, it's probably got jizz all over it now, fucking sket.

K: You're the sket—you prick—you're gonna cost us the game. We'll be a player down.

C: Can't you just play five aside?

K: No, cos if we do, it means I won't get to play. I'm meant to be Wing Attack, Cara, and you're Wing Defence. That's how it always works.

C: Yeah well, I'm going off netball.

K: You what?

C: And I can't do tonight anyways, got to see my Mum.

K: You don't want to play netball anymore?

C: It's boring, Kelly.

K: It's *everything*.

C: Yeah, for you maybe, / fucking hell.

K: What have you got to see your Mum for, then?

CARA shrugs.

K: I thought she was at that centre?

C: She was.

K: To get better.

C: Yeah, well she's not there anymore, is she?

K: So where is she living now?

C: Why are you asking so many questions?

K: I was just wondering.

C: No, you're being nosey.

K: I was just / asking.

C: Leave it, Kelly.

K: Well fuck off then.

C: Grow up.

KELLY gets out her school diary.

C: I'll make it up to you.

K: You always say that.

KELLY signs her diary with a flourish.

C: Oh sign mine please?

K: No. Not this week.

C: What? Why not?

K: I'll sign it if you play tonight.

C: Don't be a bitch.

K: Just get your Dad to sign it tonight. It's only Monday, Miss' let you off.

C: I can't.

K: Cos of your detention?

C: Such a pisstake.

K: Sorry, but saying "I couldn't be fucked" isn't a valid reason to not hand in / your homework.

C: And I can't ask my Dad tonight. He's fucked off.

K: Again?

C: Yeah.

K: Where?

C: Well if I fucking knew, I'd tell you, wouldn't I?

K: Did he not say where he was going?

C: Not this time.

KELLY puts her diary away.

K: Why don't you get your Mum to sign it then? If you can peel her off the floor.

A beat.

CARA throws her bag over her shoulder and storms off.

KELLY calls after her.

K: Oh come on Cara, I didn't mean it like that.

CARA sticks two fingers up and continues walking off-stage.

K: Yeah, whatever.

KELLY gets her Blackberry phone and begins typing, then hits enter. She swings her bag over her shoulder, and exits the stage.

II.

Saturday night. KELLY'S bedroom.

CARA and KELLY are taking photos on KELLY's laptop using the Webcam Toy website, posing with peace signs and duck faces.

C: Stop showing off your boobs.

K: I'm not.

C: You are, I can literally see you pushing them up.

K: I'm literally not. This is just how they are in this top.

C: You should change it then.

K: Why?

C: Cos it makes you look like a slag.

CARA leans forward and grabs KELLY's left breast. KELLY pushes her off.

C: They're literally massive.

K: You're just jealous.

C: I am, to be fair.

K: Lezzer.

Both girls laugh.

KELLY groans, and shouts out of her bedroom door.

K: No! We're not ready yet.

K: Five minutes!

K: It's fine, we can stick it in the microwave.

KELLY slams her bedroom door shut.

C: Your mum is well nice.

K: She's alright.

C: She's dropping us off, *and* picking us up.

K: It's only ten minutes in the car. We could literally walk, only that she'd have a fit.

C: Do you think Liam's gonna be there tonight?

K: Think so. It sounded like it on his BBM status.

KELLY gets her phone from her pocket.

CARA leaps to grab it.

K: Oi!

C: Sorry! [*reading aloud*] "Gunna b a mad 1 tnite! / YOLO."

K: You really need to ask your brother for a / Blackberry.

C: "Gunna be a / mad 1!"

K: Cos It's a bit silly / now.

C: "You Only Live / Once"

K: How much you're missing / out on.

C: I can't believe this.

K: Are you even listening to me?

C: Are you listening to *me*? Are you seeing this?

K: Who even cares, like, he's just gonna be off his face and beg for like, drugs.

C: You wouldn't get it.

K: Yeah and I don't want to. He only chats to you cos he thinks it'll get him a discount from Ben.

C: Who's being jealous now?

K: Oh fuck off.

C: No you. You can. You can fuck off. Cos this is serious, Kelly. This is like, seriously love. It's like—it feels like being on fire, I feel like someone set me on fire, it's like, everything in my body has just shifted and turned upside down. It feels like my brain is about to fall out of my labia.

K: You what?

C: It's the actual word for it, yeah? Some of us actually pay attention in sex-ed.

K: Eurgh, no thanks. I'm still traumatised from having to stick condoms on dildos.

C: They weren't dildos. They were just little plastic penises.

K: Yeah whatever. My sisters told me it'd be bananas. I was ready for bananas.

C: "Gunna b a mad 1 tnite!". Ohmigooooood.

K: You're not even going out with him, how can you love someone you're not going out with?

C: It's how I feel, Kelly. Okay? It feels like someone has taken this rope and is twisting it in my tummy and the rope is made of barbed wire and glass but it's also the best feeling ever—like being on a rollercoaster that's going up and up until you're in space, you're in the stars, and you think that you can't breathe because you're in space, but then you see that he's there, Liam's there up in the stars with you and it's like, ohmigooood, oh my God, I can breathe again. And you know, you know that he's the reason why. I see him, and I can breathe again. I see him, and I'm alive.

KELLY applies lipgloss.

K: If you become a teen mum, I'm not looking after the baby when you go out.

C: Fucking hell, I'm not.

K: Yeah well, it happens.

C: I know it happens. You think I don't know that fucking happens? I'd never do that to my kids. Alright? I'm not having a baby at 14, and I'm never gonna be on the dole, and I absolutely will never fuck off and disappear and leave my kids cos I can't even look after myself.

A beat.

KELLY's phone dings. It's time. They squeal with excitement.

KELLY takes CARA's hand. They smile.

III.

After school. Bus stop.

CARA is sat listening to music with a pair of wired earphones. KELLLY enters.

K: Oi.

> *CARA ignores KELLY.*
>
> *KELLY removes a headphone from CARA's ear.*

K: You still annoyed at me?

C: That depends.

K: On what.

C: If you're gonna apologise for being a bitch.

K: How was I being a bitch?

C: You refused to pair up with me. I looked like a right dick.

K: I thought you was gonna pair up with Liam. You said you would.

C: Yeah but he wanted to pair up with his mate. Prick.

K: How is that my fault?

C: And now I've got to do this stupid project with Alice.

K: I was trying to help you out.

C: No, you wasn't. You just didn't want to pair up with me.

K: Oh, come off it.

C: Cos you think I'm thick.

K: I don't.

C: But it's fine cos next year I'll have to take Double Science and you can fuck off to Triple Sciences with all the other specky cunts.

K: Are you done?

C: Nah. You're done.

KELLY reaches into her bag and pulls out a brown paper pouch. She hands the brown paper pouch to CARA.

CARA opens it, reaches inside, and begins to eat the snack.

KELLY takes one of CARA's headphones and begins listening to music with her. They hum to 'I Love It—Icona Pop ft, Charli XCX'.

K: Oh, I like this one.

C: It's alright.

K: I've always wanted to go on a mad one like that.

C: You can't even cross the road without asking your Mum first.

K: (*singing*) I don't care! I love it! I don't care!

The music grows, becoming louder and louder. KELLY gets up, and begins to dance.

Shortly after, she pulls up CARA who reluctantly joins in.

The music becomes distorted. The dancing of the girls becomes more erratic, taking on a hysteric quality.

CARA spots someone. The music cuts.

C: Oi. What are you staring at then?

KELLY stops dancing.

K: I can't see anyone.

C: It's cos she ran off. Fucking hell, she's well fast. Shouldn't be surprised, that lot normally are.

K: Who was it?

C: That new one in your tutor group. Sum-something.

K: Oh, Sumaya? Yeah she's weird. Never talks.

Both girls sit down again.

K: I'd hate to join halfway through term though, wouldn't you? Especially cos like, in Year 9 you basically already know everyone and all the groups are decided.

C: Yeah like, you've literally worked out who your friends are going to be like, forever, and then you've got some freak who doesn't even speak English trying to join in.

K: She does.

C: Well I've never heard it.

K: Cos she's quiet. She's probably traumatised or something.

C: Why?

K: Cos she's a refugee.

C: What? Where'd you hear that from.

K: Miss said.

C: What, like, a real one?

K: Well, I don't think she's faking it.

C: And now, she's like, living here?

K: She's probably not planning on going back.

C: Yeah, doubt it. How many siblings does she have?

KELLY shrugs.

C: I bet it's loads. All packed up in their little house like sardines.

K: Eurgh. Hate sardines.

CARA goes to skip the song on her phone.

K: No! Don't. It's a good one.

C: Her voice is annoying.

K: (*singing*) I don't know about you, but I'm feeling 22!

C: Do you think we'll still be friends at 22?

K: Obviously. I'm gonna throw you a surprise party for your birthday, and when you open the door we'll all shout "surprise!", and start playing this.

C: And I'll be like "nooooo I hate this song".

K: (*singing*) Twenty-two-oooo—

C: I'm gonna be so fit when I'm 22.

K: You're fit now.

C: No but like, I'm gonna be lethal. Tit job, nose job, permanent extensions.

K: You gonna afford all that with dole money?

C: I'll have my own money. My own business. I'll be minted.

K: Oh yeah? What's your business plan?

C: Who are you, fucking Alan Sugar? I dunno yet, alright, but it's gonna be big. God, I can't wait to get out of here.

K: I don't mind it.

C: It's a shithole.

K: Got everything you need here.

C: *You've* got everything you need. As soon as I can, I'm getting out. Leaving this place far behind.

K: Oh, thanks a lot.

C: Obviously with you. You're the one that's gonna plan all the parties, remember?

K: What type of house are you gonna have, when you're rich?

C: Proper modern one. Like all glass. And then a pool. Underground. And it'll have dogs that are my guard dogs but are also my pets, like these huge rotties.

K: Everyone's gonna see you naked if it's all glass.

C: And I'm gonna go on holiday every year, to like Jamaica and Ibiza and Tenerife, every year, twice a year, always flying off somewhere.

K: Tenerife isn't *that* nice.

C: And I'll have a bedroom with a dressing room attached, a whole room, just for my clothes, and my shoes, and my bags, and I'll have a stylist do all my shopping so it's always got new stuff. And it's all gonna be designer.

K: All designer? You'd better have Calvin Klein. C and K.

C: Obviously. (*CARA holds out her hand in a pinky promise*) You and me babe.

IV.

Lunchtime. Back gate.

CARA is smoking a cigarette. KELLY enters.

K: That from Liam then?

C: Whatever.

K: You're ruining your lungs. You know that, don't you? Turning them black. Like tar.

C: Don't care.

K: You won't be able to run. Won't be able to play netball.

C: I already told you, I've already / gone off fucking netball.

K: Gone off netball, yeah, I know. It's fine, we don't need you on the team now anyways. The new girl joined.

C: Didn't know they had netball in African war-zones.

K: She's alright.

C: Yeah? Not surprised. Sporty Spice. Or Scary. You'd better watch out.

K: She's not *that* good. I'm still the best. Well, like, in our year anyway. But Miss is being proper nice to her cos apparently we all have to suck up to her now.

C: That's how it works. They get the best treatment and we all get left in the shit.

K: What's got your back up?

C: Whatever.

A beat.

CARA stubs out her cigarette.

C: D'you want to go down to the river tonight?

K: How come?

C: Dunno. Could be fun. Got some voddy from my brother.

K: Course you did. Did you nick a gram of ket as well?

C: Nah sod that. He got so angry last time. Said I was fucking up his work. It's not worth it.

K: Oh, right. Well, I can't anyway.

C: How come?

K: I just can't.

C: What, your Mum won't let you? Fuck's sake, it's a Friday.

K: She's just like, pranging out for no reason.

C: Fucking hell, what is it now?

K: It's just like—something weird happened last night, and I told her, and I shouldn't of cos now she's being like, proper weird.

C: Is that different to normal?

K: Oh my God, can you just listen?

C: I'm listening, alright, I am, go on.

CARA gets out her school diary. KELLY flips the pages and signs it.

K: Well, basically, obviously it's like, proper dark now, at like four. Which is so fucking bleak, like coming to school in the dark and then getting home in the dark, which is so shit. Cos it's like we never get to see the sun.

KELLY gives CARA back her school diary.

C: Yeah, I know, like it's prison.

K: Exactly. Like it's literally prison. I bet we'd see more sun in prison as well. Don't you have a cousin in Belmarsh*? He'd know.

C: Fuck off.

K: Sorry, I actually wasn't trying to be a dick, I just thought, well obviously you know—

C: Fuck *off* Kelly.

CARA moves to leave.

K: Wait, alright I'm sorry—okay? I actually am, cos like prison isn't funny.

C: It's not.

K: Yeah, no, obviously I know. But what I'm saying is like, so the thing is—yesterday after school, right, I was walking home from the bus stop. And you know how the walk back to mine goes through that weird woodland bit—

C: Yeah, it's so creepy. Dunno why you live in the middle of fucking nowhere.

K: Yeah I'd much rather be in town, like you.

CARA laughs.

C: What, you'd rather be above the chippy? Fuck off.

K: I would! But anyway like, I was walking back and I swear, there was this man that was behind me. And he was like in a hood, but you know, doesn't mean he's dodgy, but he had this like, aura? He looked proper shifty, right, yeah I think he was like Indian or whatever, so then my spider-senses were tingling—

CARA laughs.

K: No seriously, I started sweating, like proper sweating. And then I started walking faster, but then he started walking faster and I'm thinking, oh shit, oh shit, he's actually like, and he's like near me now, so then I start running, and he starts running as well, and I'm like shit, oh my God shit he's chasing, like he's actually chasing me, but I'm running fast enough to make a gap, and then Mrs Blake, you know Mrs Blake, the one one that lives down the road, she's walking her dog, her crusty white Yorkie, and I turn the corner and run straight into her and we both like fall to the floor, and I swear to God, I swear to fucking God I've never been so glad to see that shitty little crusty dog in my entire life, and I'm trying to speak but I'm panting too hard, and yeah I'm crying a bit cos it was so scary, Cara, I literally thought he was going to— anyway, I'm trying to tell Mrs Blake, but she holds me for a bit, and I turn around and he's gone, like actually gone, but his footprints are still there—I checked later and they were still there—and I'm not crazy cos he was chasing me Cara, he was definitely chasing me. And then she took me home, and she's sat having a cup of tea with my Mum, and so I have to tell them, sort of, not everything, not like I'm telling you now cos my Mum would fully prang out then and I'd be like, stuck in the house until I was 30, but yeah now my Mum is picking me up after school until next term. Cos—yeah. Mad, innit?

Long beat.

C: Good thing you ran.

K: Yeah?

C: Yeah. Got to trust our instincts, haven't we?

A beat.

C: Right. I'm gonna go.

K: Yeah, we've got English now.

C: Nah, I'm gonna *go.*

K: What, you're leaving? Is someone picking you up?

C: I'll be by the river.

K: Oh... okay. Well what do I tell Miss?

C: Tell her to stick Hamlet up her ratty little vag. I'll see you later, yeah?

K: Oh... yeah. Yeah, alright. I'll see you.

CARA leaves the stage.

KELLY looks at her hands, scuffed and bruised.

V.

Saturday night. CARA's bedroom.

The girls are eating fish and chips.

K: Feels weird.

C: What?

K: Having fish and chips on a Saturday.

C: Well sorry.

K: No—I didn't mean—

C: Didn't have to feed you at all, did I?

K: Well, to be fair, it's not like you did though, is it? Cos this is just the order that never got picked up.

KELLY gets out her Blackberry.

K: Ohmigooood look, everyone is so gassed about yesterday.

C: Yeah, it was alright.

K: Nah it was so sick, Liam's actually so funny.

C: Yeah, when he wants to be.

K: Can't believe we have to go back to school on Monday.

C: That is normally how it works.

K: I just want to do that forever, like, everyday. Like this is what we were made to do. Fuck school, and fuck having to get a job and work in a shitty little office until I'm 60 or whatever.

C: Rather an office than in a chippy.

K: I wouldn't mind it. Get free food.

C: It's not free if it's your shop though, cos you're still buying all the stuff.

K: Why do you even care? Haven't you got your big business plan?

C: Whatever.

K: Oh my God remember when Alice like, got out that stick and started running around with it—

C: She's such a freak—

K: And she was like running telling Liam she was gonna shove it up his—

C: Why did you bring her along?

K: Because she's fun, Cara. Remember that? Fun?

C: I'm fun.

K: When you want to be.

C: What's that supposed to mean?

K: I'm just saying, like I snuck out for you—

C: I never made you.

K: Well, you made it seem like I had to go.

C: You never *had* to go. Just cos you went doesn't mean you *had* to. Cos what else would you have done? Watched Corrie on the telly with your Mum?

K: Whatever. I'm just saying, I snuck out for something that you planned, and you ended up just like, being off the whole time.

C: Off?

K: Just quiet. I dunno. Thanks for the voddy though.

C: Yeah? You're fucking welcome.

A beat.

C: It's cos of that girl.

K: What girl?

C: New girl.

K: What, Sumaya? She's got a name, you know?

C: Well, I can't say it.

K: Soo—may—/—ya.

C: I don't give a fuck how you say it, Kelly. Why was she even there like, who asked for her to be there?

K: There was loads of us—

C: Yeah of *our* lot.

K: You the club bouncer now?

C: I swear I saw her drinking some of my voddy as well.

K: What, do you think she backwashed?

C: Yeah, we're all gonna catch AIDS or something now. Who even told her it was happening?

K: Could have been Liam, cos he's her science partner now.

C: No, he'd never. He wouldn't. He never chose her to be his partner as well, Sir assigned them. Cos she had no one.

K: Dunno then. Maybe she saw it on someone's BBM status.

C: As if she's got a fucking Blackberry, Wouldn't be surprised, everyone in her family probably got given one along with their free house.

K: You've got a free house, you div. Or flat, anyway.

C: Yeah, cos I've got a right to. It's what Dad always said. If you keep sharing it, you're not gonna have enough for the people that actually deserve it. In the end, we're all gonna have to go without.

K: Council will come knocking at your door.

C: Like, no offence, but, even if she wasn't—you know—she's just... weird. Too quiet. Like school shooter vibes.

K: Oh yeah? Where's she hiding the gun then? Under her hijab?

C: Exactly. You get it.

The two girls are laughing.

K: Imagine like, you're in Maths, and she just whips it out, like gets out a fucking machine gun and starts blowing up the place.

C: Nah she's got a bomb under there, swear.

K: God I hope she does't set it off in Tutor. Cos we're on the same table, like I'd be done for.

KELLY is laughing. CARA is not.

C: So fucked though, that someone can just do that.

K: What, blow you up?

C: Just kill you. Because they want to. Whenever they want to. Like that man, from the other / day.

K: Can we not talk about / him?

C: I'm just saying, like, what have the police done? Fuck all. They couldn't be arsed. They never are, when it's that lot. And now he's probably gonna do it to someone else.

K: I don't want to talk about / him.

C: But it's not about him, I'm just saying that like, we're alive, you know, like we're alive right now and that's good, it's good if you want to see it as good, but it's probably better than being dead. But being dead is so close to being alive. Do you not think about it? And us, like, young people, like, dying, I dunno. Cos old people dying is like, whatever, you're old and wrinkly and you've lived your life, so who cares. Not saying no one cares, cos obviously it was really sad when my Nan died—

K: Yeah that was well sad.

C: Yeah it was shit as well cos then Mum got really... anyways, what I'm saying is that it was sad, yeah, but it wasn't like, weird. But when you think about it, we could die at like, any time. There's nothing that says we have to actually grow old. Or any older than this. This could be it. And someone could be the person that decides that. Like not randomly, like if you got struck by lightning or got cancer or whatever. Someone could wake up one day and think, I'm going to take this away from you, I'm going to take this life away from you now, and you'll have nothing. You'll be dead, which is a sort of nothing. And that person could be yourself. Or someone else. A terrorist, a man chasing you in the woods, or it could be by accident, which is almost worse in a way, cos like. Imaging dying from someone else's accident.

K: Yeah, that'd be so shit.

C: And sometimes I think about it, like not on purpose. But like I'll just be watching telly or walking to school or whatever, and then I'll just get this random thought, like this random wave of—I dunno—like fear? I think, but not at anything specifically, just at the thought of it. And sometimes it's really graphic, like someone stabbing me, and I think I can feel it? Sometimes, I swear I can feel it, like that pain, that pain that comes before the nothing, and it's like, I shouldn't have to think about that.

I shouldn't have to be scared like that, but I am. Cos that's the world we live in, now.

CARA lies down.

KELLY holds her hand.

K: (*softly*) You'd better not die.

C: I'm not planning on it.

KELLY lies down next to CARA.

K: Good. Cos I'd have to kill you if you ever planned on leaving me.

C: Fuck off, that's so gay. Why are you so obsessed with me?

CARA holds KELLY's hand. They stay like that.

VI.

Lunchtime. Lunch hall.

C: Oh my God, Kelly, I'm literally going to shit myself and die.

K: No same. Literally. Same.

C: Oh my God. Ohmigooood. Oh my fucking God.

K: I know.

C: This actually might just be the best day of my entire fucking life.

K: I knowwwww—just wait until the actual concert.

C: McBusted. Fucking McFly. And Busted.

K: I. Know.

C: Happy fucking birthday!

K: I think it's her way of saying sorry, for like, not letting me have a party.

C: Oh my God I might faint. My heart's going so fast. Feel.

CARA puts KELLY's hand to her chest.

K: Oh my God, Cara, you're gonna have a fucking heart attack. Stop it.

C: I can't, I can't, I'm gonna die, I'm literally gonna die, right here, right now, on the spot, and then I'll have to go to the concert / as a ghost.

K: Also—also, don't shit yourself, but look.

KELLY gets out a pink iPhone 5c from her pocket.

C: What. The. Fuck.

K: I know.

C: It's only just come out.

K: I know—I'm moving up in the world.

C: Oh my God, you lucky bitch.

K: Blackberries are out. iPhones are in. Slag.

K: You can have my old one if you want.

C: No point now, if everyone's getting rid of theirs.

K: Still there if you want it.

C: Yeah thanks. Whatever.

K: D'you want to have a go?

CARA shrugs, 'go on'. KELLY hands over the iPhone. KELLY looks around half-smug, then stops short.

K: Shit.

C: What?

CARA looks up in the direction KELLY is facing.

K: Shit.

C: Oh my God.

K: It's fine, Cara.

C: What the fuck.

K: It's probably nothing.

C: Why the fuck is he sat with her?

K: It's actually not that deep.

C: He barely fucking speaks to me for three days, and now he's sat with that freak at lunch? What the fuck are they even talking about?

K: Probably just the stuff from science. You know how thick he is, he's probably just like, making her do his homework or whatever,

C: Liam doesn't care about that shit, you know that.

K: Yeah, maybe he's changed his mind.

C: They're *laughing*. Fucking laughing it up, and you think they're talking about fucking mitochondria?

K: He'd never go for her. You know that.

C: I don't.

K: Yeah you do!

C: No, I fucking don't.

K: Fine, but I do. Like seriously. Fucking hell, Look at her. And look at you. You're so hot. She's a fucking freak. She's a weirdo. No one talks to her. No one fucking can, cos she hardly understands what anyone says. Right? Cara! Cara, listen to me, you're the fittest girl in our year. And she's nobody. She's nothing. It's literally not a comparison.

C: I thought you liked her.

K: She's not *you*, Cara. Obviously.

C: I'm gonna go over.

K: No you're not.

C: I am.

K: That's just what he wants. He's probably just doing this to wind you up.

C: Do you think so?

K: Definitely. Right, just leave it.

C: They're probably laughing at me.

K: Don't.

C: Laughing at the photos I sent him, that he fucking asked for.

K: They're not.

C: Look, they're looking at his phone. She's practically leaning over him.

K: Yeah but he's leaning away. Sort of.

C: She thinks she's better than me. She does. She thinks I'm a slag. I know it.

K: Who cares what she thinks?

C: She does. Cos it's in their culture, you know.

K: I know. It's fucked.

C: They hate women showing—

K: Tits.

C: Any types of freedom.

K: It's the law.

C: It's in their Bible.

K: Quran.

C: Bitch.

K: Cara.

C: Fucking bitch.

K: Look he's leaving her.

C: Yeah, only cos his boys have come over.

K: And he's embarrassed.

C: He's such a prick.

K: I've always said.

C: Nah, you said he was funny.

K: Yeah. But he's still a prick.

A beat.

K: Oh—he's looking at us.

C: Yeah?

K: Shit, Cara he's—oh, nevermind—sorry, I thought he was—

C: It's fine.

K: Sorry, I didn't mean to—

C: I said it's fine, alright? Don't want to fucking speak to him anyways.

K: Yeah, yeah whatever. He can fuck off and all.

A beat.

CARA begins to cry.

C: Oh for fuck's sake.

K: Cara?

C:...

K: You alright?

C: No I'm not fucking alright.

K: Sorry.

KELLY pulls in a reluctant CARA for a hug.

C: It's just shit, you know?

K: Yeah, I know.

KELLY pulls back and holds CARA by the shoulders.

K: Right.

C: Yeah?

K: You know what you've got to do?

C: What?

K: You need to start chirpsing someone else.

C: But I don't want anyone else.

K: That literally doesn't matter. Alright? It's not about what you want, it's about what you have to do.

C: Who though?

K: Neil?

C: But they're best friends.

K: Exactly. Can you imagine how fucked off you'd be if I started shacking up with Liam? If I stole your boyfriend off you?

C: Yeah... but didn't you already do that?

K: Cara.

C: Like I haven't got to imagine, when it actually fucking happened.

K: Cara, for fuck's sake.

C: Cos I still remember, you know. How shit that felt. That backstabbing bullshit.

K: It was literally years ago.

C: Cos me and Colin were holding hands at break time, and look, guess who's snogging him by lunch.

K: It was kiss chase.

C: It was a betrayal.

K: We were eight years old.

C: And that's where I learned what true heartbreak was.

K: Fine.

C: And now I've got to go through it again.

K: Fucking fine.

C: And you don't even care.

K: I do care, Cara. I do. And I'm sorry—OK? I'm sorry for what happened five—fucking, six years ago. And I'm sorry that it's still hurting you today. I am. But look at you. You can't do this. You can't let him win. Right? The best thing for you to do, yeah, is for you to hold your head up high, and say: yeah, I sent you a photo of my tits, and yeah, you stopped talking to me cos you think I'm flat, and yeah, I do feel really used, and really horrible, but do you know what? You've got to say: I can get that power back. We can, Cara. We're the ones that can stop fucking caring, and just do whatever we want.

C: Yeah.

K: Alright?

C: Yeah. Fine. I can chirpse Neil, or whatever.

K: Exactly.

C: But it's not just him though.

K: Yeah?

C: It's not just Liam, is it? Takes two to tango.

K: Right.

C: I don't care about him not wanting to go out with me. Well I do—yeah, obviously—but leaving me for her?

K: He's not.

C: Well he won't. I'll make sure of that.

K: How?

C: Dunno yet. But I'm going to sort this out.

K: *We're* gonna sort this out.

A beat.

C: What have you got now?

K: Drama. You've got Food Tech.

C: Oh fuuuuuck shit. I haven't got my fucking Demerara sugar.

K: Oh shit!

C: It's fine. Whatever. You probably don't need it for apple crumble do you?

K: Nah. No. Don't think so.

C: See you after, yeah?

K: Yeah, see you.

C: Oh and Kels—

K: Yeah?

CARA holds KELLY by the sides of her head.

C: Happy birthday.

CARA kisses KELLY on the cheek, and leaves the stage. KELLY leaves in the opposite direction.

VII.

After school. CARA's living room.

The girls are watching 'Twilight' on television.

K: I'll stop taking about it.

C: No, it's alright.

K: I will.

C: Well. It has been like, two days.

K: Yeah.

C: Non-stop.

K: Sorry. It's just shit.

C: I know, yeah. You said.

> *A beat. They watch the television.*

K: Did I tell you, they found the man that chased me.

C: No, you didn't. Too busy going on about netball.

K: Yeah. Sorry.

C: How?

K: Apparently he flashed Alice in a park but her brother was there and he fucked him up.

C: How do you know it was him though?

K: Saw a picture of him on her Facebook. At least, I think it was him.

C: Probably was. Are you gonna get the bus now then?

K: Don't think so. Mum still wants to give me lifts.

C: Oh.

K: I wish I had a brother.

C: No, you don't.

K: Well, not one like yours.

C: What's that supposed to mean?

K: No, it's just like. Well, he's not the most, like, caring, is he?

C: Ben's looked after me more than you'll ever know. More than my Dad, probably.

K: Definitely more than your Mum.

A beat.

K: Have you heard from him yet?

C: Who?

K: Your Dad.

C: Oh. No.

K: Oh. It's been months now.

C: Have you been counting?

K: No.

A beat. They watch the film.

K: Has Neil replied to you yet?

C: No. I don't think he's that bothered, to be honest.

K: He's clapped anyways.

C: Yeah.

A beat. They watch the film.

K: At least Bella never had to deal with this shit.

C: Yeah. She was too busy trying to get off with a hundred-year old vampire.

A beat. They watch the film.

K: It's just. Sorry, I know I keep going on about it, but it's just shit, you know?

CARA shifts slightly. She's heard this before. A lot.

K: It's just like, you try so fucking hard, And it's like. What's the point. What's the fucking point? I've been there every week, every week I've been there, since Year 7. Every shitting Wednesday, even in the pissing rain. And extra sessions too, before matches. Because it's important. And yeah, I know you might not think so, but it is, it's important to me, Cara. It's not just a game. Like, when you're on the court, and the match starts, everything just shifts into gear. Everything thing else falls away. It's about you, your team and that ball. That stupid fucking ball. That's all it is. And she's taken that away from me.

C: And you deserved it.

K: I know. I was so good, Cara. I was brilliant, I am fucking brilliant. And it's like, what's the point, you know. All those years. It was meant to be my team, Cara. Mine. Next year, it was meant to be mine. But then Louise had to go and tear her ACL, and Miss doesn't even replace her with another girl in Year 10 as captain. She gives it to that fucking bitch. New girl. And she's not even that good. Like she's fine, she's alright, but you can tell she doesn't even try. She doesn't practice like I do. And she isn't even there every week. Cos she has to look after her rancid little brothers. She's not even committed. And Miss makes her captain instead. Her. Over me.

C: Well, what are you gonna do about it then?

K: Quit, probably.

C: You're not gonna do that.

K: Oh, so you can tell me what to do now?

C: I can actually, and I'm telling you, right now, you're not gonna quit.

K: What, so I just keep playing under her team? For the next two years? I don't fucking think so.

C: No, you won't. I know you, Kelly. You're not gonna quit. And Sumaya won't be captain for long, I'll tell you that fucking much.

They are interrupted by a phone call.

K: Shit.

C: What.

K: It's my Mum.

C: Well, take it then?

K: Yeah, don't pause it.

KELLY runs off stage answering the call. CARA watches the television.

She snorts.

C: Daft sparkly cunt.

CARA watches the television.

A few moments later, KELLY runs back on stage in a panic.

K: Fuck.

C: You alright?

K: No. Shit. Fuck. It's all fucked.

C: What happened?

K: My Mum—she—she's really angry.

C: That's new.

K: No—it's serious. This is fucking serious.

C: OK?

K: FUCK!

C: Kelly!

K: So you know how with like the iPhones and stuff, you've got this thing called iCloud.

C: Wait slow down, what cloud?

K: iCloud.

C: Right.

K: And it's like what you have to make when you get a phone, you've got to make an account—listen to me—and then you're meant to link it across like other devices, like iPods or computers or whatever—

C: Kelly, fucking hell—I feel like I'm in an ICT lesson.

K: I don't know how she saw it—I must have logged in somewhere—at some point—

C: What are you on about?

K: She's seen all my messages, Cara.

C: What?

K: All of my texts. On the computer. From my phone. It's linked to my cloud, my fucking iCloud thing.

C: Oh.

K: Yeah.

C: That's not good.

K: I know.

C: Fuck.

K: Yeah. Cos. It was just messages, like, they were just texts, I wasn't actually going to do anything.

C: Yeah.

K: Fuck.

C: Well you were really upset.

K: Yeah.

C: About not being made captain.

K: I was.

C: It's not your fault.

K: Yeah?

C: If anything, it's Miss Wilson's fault, for not making you captain. When you obviously deserved it.

K: I've never heard her so angry.

C: Shit.

K: She said she couldn't believe I'd send messages like that. That I'd embarrass her like that.

C: God, bit fucking dramatic. Why's she so fucking dramatic?

K: And she said—she said—

C: What? What is it?

K: She said I can't go—that *we* can't go to the concert.

A beat.

C: FUCK.

K: I know.

C: She can't do that.

K: She can.

C: Oh my God.

K: I'm gonna go home.

C: You have to convince her.

K: I'll try. I will.

C: It's your birthday present.

K: I know.

C: It's not fair.

K: It's not.

C: They were just messages. Telling her how it is. How she didn't deserve to be captain. How it's not fair that she's getting fucking handed everything, when you work so fucking hard.

K: I know.

C: And that she's a fucking rag-head bitch.

K: Was that too far?

C: No. Maybe. No.

K: Fuck. That was your fucking idea.

C: No it wasn't.

K: Yes it was. *You* typed it out.

C: Well, you're the one that sent it? Alright? It came from your fucking phone.

K: Oh my God, what are we going to do?

C: I don't knowwww, I don't know.

K: Fuck, I should go.

C: Text me, yeah?

K: I can't. She says she's going to take away my phone.

C: She can't do that.

K: Yeah?

C: Yeah. It's like abuse. It's fucking child abuse. You can ring Childline, you know?

K: I can't. Not without a phone.

C: Shit! Shit. What are you gonna do?

K: It's fine. It's fine. It's fine, I'll sort it. I'll beg.

C: Please.

K: I will. I will.

KELLY runs off stage.

CARA stares at the television for a few moments alone, then turns it off.

VIII.

Saturday afternoon. Outside.

CARA is chewing frantically on a piece of gum.

C: I swear, like, your aunt's a lawyer isn't she?

K: Yeah, for like, land and taxes and stuff, not for this.

C: Yeah, like, but she knows people?

K: I dunno, maybe.

C: So she can help?

K: It's a different type of law, Cara.

C: Yeah but like, he doesn't have anyone. Right now. And he needs someone. Anything is better than nothing.

K: Cara, my Mum isn't even talking to me. She's icing me out. It's fucking horrible.

C: Just because your Mum's a fucking psycho doesn't mean you can't help me.

K: Yeah but I've got to ask her—

C: Why? Why've you got to get her involved in everything?

K: Because it's her sister. And all I have is this fucking Nokia brick. Thanks to you. So I can't speak to anyone properly even if I wanted to.

C: Right, so you've got to steal your phone back then.

K: Oh for fuck's sake.

C: She can't have hidden it that well. You've just got to fucking look.

K: Cara—

C: Kelly. My brother has just been nicked. And right now, there's fuck all I can do, except for this. OK? So just try to fucking help me.

K: Isn't he meant to get a solicitor, or something? From the government?

C: You what?

K: The government have to help him. It's the law.

C: The government aren't going to do shit, Kelly. They don't give a fuck about people like us. They don't care, and you know that.

K: I just think you're being a bit—I mean—they haven't actually arrested him cos of the drugs—

C: Yeah / but—

K: Like, technically, it was actually sort of his own / fault—

C: They're gonna keep digging and digging and then / it's—

K: Like, I just think if he didn't want to get into shit, then why would he go onto the estate? You lot don't even live there.

C: It's not about where we fucking live. Right, they were the ones that started it. Posting on Snapchat and calling him a pussy, when he's not. And he had to show them. All of his boys did.

K: And where are his boys now?

C: For fuck's sake, Kelly.

K: I'm just saying, like, this is just like you. All of this. Making me run around—It's like what happened with your Mum, when you made / me—

C: I never made you do / anything—

K: When you asked me to get money from my Mum, basically stealing, and to tell her I had a fucking geography / trip—

C: You didn't want to go on that fucking trip / anyways—

K: You had me lie to her, write out a fake fucking letter—

C: You hate camping, you always / said—

K: Staying at yours for a whole weekend, all so you could let your Mum keep using.

C: And if she went off cold turkey it could've killed her. Is that what you want?

K: I'm not saying that.

C: And she's better now so it was actually—

K: Well she's not, is she?

C: Oh fuck you.

K: Well, sorry, but she's not. You can keep telling yourself that she is but I've seen her hanging out at the top of town again looking like, I dunno...

C: Like what? Like what, Kelly?

K: God. Looking like a fucking smackhead. Is that what you want me to say?

A beat.

C: You're a fucking ratty bitch.

K: I am? Me? After everything I've done? Are you taking the piss?

C: What have *you* done? You help me a few times and think you can make me into your fucking charity case—

K: You're not my charity / case—

C: When I'm the one that has to deal with all of this? What would you know about anything? You haven't got a fucking clue what it's like.

K: For fuck's sake. It's always like this with you. It's always about *you*. It's always about your life, and your problems, and all your shit going on, and I'm just meant to go along with it. And I'm bored. It's boring, Cara. And the thing is, you think it makes you so interesting. Like, you have all this shit and it's almost like you're proud of it, you're proud of it cos you get to walk around and be the person that everyone's, like, talking about, and your brother, you say you want me to help him but I think, I think secretly you love it. I think you love that he's dealing, I think you love that he's in trouble with the police, and you love that everyone's scared of him, cos it makes you feel important. It makes you feel like somebody.

CARA moves to leave.

K: And you're gonna storm off now, cos you don't want to hear the truth. You're gonna make me out to be the bitch, when it's the people in your fucking family that are the fucking problem, right, when it's your fucking brother that's dealing to your fucking Mum. God, it's no wonder you turned out like this.

A beat.

CARA runs back onstage and launches at KELLY.

The two have a fight. It's dirty. Ratty. Biting, hair pulling, smacking. Neither are very good. CARA is more aggressive but KELLY is more athletic.

Eventually, it's a stalemate. They both sit on the floor. Heavy breathing. Then, silence.

K: I'm sorry.

C: No.

K: I am.

C: No. *No.* This isn't right. This isn't *us*, Kel.

K: I know. It's just been... so much. Recently.

KELLY leans her head on CARA's shoulder.

CARA begins to cry, then aggressively wipes away her tears.

C: Fuck's sake.

K: I'll call her. I can do. If that's what you want, I will. I know where she's hidden it. She sneaks it out to play Candy Crush, and thinks I don't know.

C: No, no it's alright. Not today. Let him spend the night in the nick. Maybe it'll stop him from acting like such a cunt.

K: But tomorrow?

C: Yeah, tomorrow.

K: You know I love you, right?

C: I know.

A beat.

C: I love you too.

K: I know.

C: I'm telling you, Kelly, this isn't us.

K: We've had rows before.

C: Yeah but, not like that. Not that nasty.

K: It never used to be like this.

C: It didn't.

CARA strokes KELLY's hair.

K: Have you decided on your choices yet? We've only got a week.

C: You know what Sir said the other day?

K: What?

C: He thinks I should do Triple Sciences.

K: You're joking?

C: Don't sound so surprised.

K: I'm not.

C: Someone here doesn't think I'm thick as shit.

K: You're not. I've never thought that.

C: Thanks.

K: So, are you gonna do it?

C: Maybe. If I can be arsed. Think it'll be a waste of time?

K: Not if we're together.

C: Don't be gay.

K: I'm not.

A beat.

K: I told my Mum I hated her last night.

C: Yeah?

K: I just kept screaming it: "I hate you, I hate YOU, I HATE YOU, I HATE YOU."

C: You're mental.

K: ...

C: Maybe you're losing it.

K: ...

C: Maybe we both are.

A beat.

C: When the police came round, Ben was sat on the sofa. He was just sat there, chilling, on his Playstation. And I was in my room, with the door open. And I was thinking about you, and the concert, and how everything just feels like it's going to shit now, and I was thinking about what we could do, and then they stormed in, with this huge, door buster thing, smashed the door right through, which is stupid because they didn't even knock—it was just "armed police" and then they split the door in two. And I thought, you might as well knock, you might as well have cos I would've just let you in, probably would've offered you a cuppa and all. But they bashed it through and he was just sat there in his pants, on the sofa that I'm not allowed to sit on when he's in the house. And obviously, cos he's an idiot, he started mouthing off, and they told him to get on the floor but he didn't, he didn't cos he kept saying it's my house, "it's my fucking house and I can stand if I want", and then they got him on the floor and one of them was twisting his arm, and he kept screaming my arm, "that fucking hurts, my arm" and then this woman came over, this lady police officer, and she was smiling and being proper nice, and then shut the door so I couldn't see anything, which was annoying because I wanted to see, I wanted to know. Not that I felt sorry for him. They wouldn't have kicked him if he wasn't being a prick. But this lady was smiling and asking me where my parents were. And I said that my Dad had fucked off, and my Mum wasn't about, and then I asked her if they were gonna replace the bloody door they just tore off, and then she laughed at me, and I said "it wasn't fucking funny" and she stopped laughing. Wiped the smile off her face there didn't I? And then she said she couldn't leave me in the house alone, not without a parent or guardian present, and I thought it was funny she thought that Ben was any type of guardian. Funny that. Probably safer without him there. So then I did ask her, I asked her if she wanted a cuppa, and we were in the kitchen and they'd taken Ben out, they must have taken him out in just his pants and I thought of how cold he'd be in the back of a police van. And I made her a cuppa and she was just sat there, on the phone to the council or something, and I told her I had to go for a wee but our toilet was downstairs, next to the chippy, and she said alright, "alright love, I'll just be here", and then I went, ran out, out, out of the broken door, out of the stairwell, and out here. And there you were. There you were, Kelly.

A beat.

K: Is she gonna be looking for you?

CARA laughs.

C: No one's gonna be looking for me.

K: Do you want to come round to mine?

CARA shakes her head.

C: I'm gonna see about fixing the door. Gonna get cold otherwise.

K: How are you gonna do that?

C: I'll sort it. Get a shower curtain if I have to.

The girls hug.

They break apart. CARA prevents them from fully separating, and puts their heads together. There is electricity shared between their skulls.

They break apart fully.

C: Today.

K: Yeah?

C: We do it today.

K: Right.

C: We're just gonna talk to her, before the others arrive.

K: Yeah? Are you sure?

C: Kelly. Think about it. Think about how fucked everything is, now, because of her.

K: We'll just talk to her, tell her to back off Liam, and then get her to tell Miss that she isn't ready to be captain—

C: We can even get her to speak to your Mum or something, after school. And make her say it was a joke. That's all it was, those messages, a fucking joke. Tell her that we just did it for a laugh.

K: Yeah.

C: And then she'll fuck off, and the others will get there, we can all hang out by the river like we always do.

K: Like we always do.

C: And it'll be normal again.

K: And I'll get my phone back.

C: And we'll see McBusted.

K: And things will be–

C: Good. They're gonna be good, Kels.

K: Okay... I can, um, I can bring some of my Mum's wine.

C: Yeah, and I'll text the others.

K: Shit.

C: It'll work.

K: Yeah?

C: Yeah.

K: Okay. Okay!

C: I'll bring some of my brother's stuff—

K: Yeah?

C: Yeah. Not like he needs it, right now.

K: Cool.

C: I know where he hides it.

K: Under the floorboards.

C: Rip it up.

K: It'll be good.

C: Yeah. Put us in the mood.

K: In the right—

C: Headspace.

K: And it'll be done.

C: Yeah.

K: Done.

C: Don't be scared.

K: I'm not. I'm not.

The girls shake hands. It's a silly, choreographed handshake that they've been doing for years. Afterwards, they stay holding each others hands. They hug.

CARA leaves.

KELLY leaves in the other direction. She turns around, like she wants to say something, but the stage is empty. She looks out, to the audience, as if she has noticed them. She is spooked.

KELLY leaves the stage.

IX.

After.

Near the river.

KELLY runs on stage. CAR follows shortly after. It is dark.

They are missing some of their clothes.

K: FuckfuckfuckfuckfuckfuckfuckFUCK.

C: Kelly—

K: OhmyGod, Oh my God, Oh my fucking—

C: Kelly, where are you?

K: What the fuck, what the actual—

Lights up.

C: There you are, for fuck's sake.

K: Don't touch me! Don't you fucking touch me.

C: I'm not going to—fine—fine—OK, fine—

K: Oh my God—What the fuck—

C: Fucking hell, did you see that? Did you fucking see that?

K: Of course I fucking saw it—I was there—

C: Oh my God you're soaking—

K: So are you—so are YOU—

C: Shit yeah, I am. God, it's fucking freezing—

K: Where is she? Where the fuck is she?

C: She's in the water—she's in the water Kelly—

K: Well we have to—we have to get her out—

C: We can't. We can't touch her.

K: Fuck. FUCK. What the fuck—

C: Kelly you need to—

K: What the fuck have we done—nononononono—

C: For fuck's sake, can you just—

K: If you tell me to calm down I'll actually—

C: No—no—you actually—you need to shut the fuck up.

KELLY starts.

K: Sorry—what?

C: Stop fucking panicking, okay?

K: No, we need to—we need to go back—we need to go and—

C: We can't go back. There is no going back.

K: Then we need to—shit—fuck—okay—we need to—

C: Kelly, it's done. Okay? She's not moving.

K: We were just meant to talk to her. You said we'd just fucking talk to her.

C: We did. We did try that, but she wasn't listening.

K: I didn't think she'd—

C: Neither did I.

K: Oh my God I think I'm going to be sick—

C: I've called the ambulance.

K: You *what?*

C: Well what the fuck did you want me to do? She was fucking floating.

K: What did you do? What did you fucking do?

KELLY shoves CARA.

C: Me? What did you fucking do?

CARA shoves KELLY.

K: No I—I didn't—I didn't mean to—

C: Oh yeah? Cos if I remember correctly, it was you that told her to go in the water.

K: No, I—I never—

C: You who pulled her in, even though she didn't want to.

K: I thought she was joking—I didn't know she couldn't—and she was dragging me under—you saw, you saw it—oh my God—

C: If you're gonna be sick, don't do it near me.

K: What are we gonna do? What the fuck are we going to do?

C: We tell them what happened.

K: What?

C: We went in, she joined us. She couldn't swim. We tried to pull her out, but she was too heavy. Too much fabric. Too many layers.

K: Do you think they'll believe it?

C: It's the truth.

K: Right.

C: And she'd taken stuff.

K: Yeah, that *you* made her swallow.

C: Yeah well, it doesn't really matter now, does it? Isn't this is what we wanted?

K: No—no—no—I—I never wanted this.

C: Why did you pull her in then? Why did you tell her you were gonna hold on to her, and you fucking let her go?

K: You could've done something—you could've—you just stood there, and watched it happen—

C: So did you.

K: Oh God—oh my fucking—I want to go home.

C: Kelly, come here.

CARA reaches out for KELLY.

KELLY pulls away, but CARA does so again, determined.

KELLY relents, and begins to cry.

C: It's alright. We'll be alright. Yeah? But we can't panic now. Cos if we do, we're fucked. My life is fucked. Your life is fucked.

K: It wasn't just me—it wasn't—you were behind her—you pushed her into—

C: It was an accident. So we've just—got to get on with the rest of it now.

KELLY's phone begins to ring.

C: Who is it?

KELLY shows CARA the contact.

C: Just tell her what happened. Alright? Can't change it now.

KELLY picks up the phone.

K: Mum?

KELLY breaks down in a sob.

K: Mum, I need your help. Something really really, really, really, really bad has happened.

X.

Shortly after. Inside.

Split stage.

The girls are sat facing forwards.

Each line of dialogue immediately follows the previous. They do not react to one another.

C: So it's being filmed then?

K: Around four I think. I don't know. Sorry.

C: Will I get to see it after?

K: Some of our friends were meant to come, a bit later. We were just gonna meet up first, just us three.

C: No, doesn't matter. Just thought I'd ask.

K: She was my... friend. We were all friends. We tried really hard to make her feel welcome.

C: I didn't know her that well, but she was alright. Kelly was the one that was properly friends with her. They played netball together.

K: She was good. Really good. Like... the best. One of the best. I don't know what we'll do without her.

C: We just went in. I don't know. I thought, we thought it would be fun. We normally do. You know, she didn't tell us she couldn't swim. I don't know why.

K: She didn't want to take her clothes off. Cos of the boys. That were joining us. Later. That's what she said. We didn't want to force her—we would never do that.

C: After she got in, the layers of her fabric started to pull her under.

K: And we tried. We kept trying to pull her out. But she went under, she went under and we were trying, but it was so hard, and she didn't... we couldn't... sorry. I'm really sorry.

C: She'd started panicking, and thrashing around. It was pulling all of us under.

K: The water was burning my lungs. I was really frightened. I couldn't see anything. And all I could hear was just shouting. All of us, just screaming.

C: I just kept thinking, I have to get back to the bank, I have to. And when I did, I saw Kelly there. She went back in for her, the second time, you know? She didn't just give up. I wanted to. But I kept being sick. There was so much water.

K: After making sure Cara was safe, I went back in for Sumaya. I kept diving in and out, but I couldn't see her. And when I did... she was down river. It was too late.

C: We tried. We really did. I'm really sorry.

K: Thank you. I don't feel very brave.

C: Yes, it has been a really overwhelming day.

K: Yeah, alright. Can I see my Mum now? I need to see my Mum.

C: I think I just want to go home. Is that OK? I just want to go home.

XI.

A week later. Outside.

C: Hey.

K: Oh. Hey.

C: You avoiding me then?

K: No.

C: Well. I haven't seen you in like, a week.

K: Five days.

C: A week.

K: ...

C: You haven't been at school.

K: What did you say?

　　A beat.

C: Same as you, I suppose.

K: Oh. OK.

C: Gonna tell me why you've been bunking off then?

K: ...

C: Didn't you hear?

K: What?

C: They want to give us some medal thing. For bravery. At school.

K: Right.

C: Thought you'd be gassed.

K: Well, I'm not.

C: I am. I'm well pleased. Never get awarded things.

K: Saw your brother out on the high street.

C: Oh, is it? Yeah. He's out on bail or something. Our Ben.

K: Well. That's good.

C: Council gave us a new door and all.

K: Didn't have to go for the shower curtain then?

C: No.

A beat. KELLY looks uncomfortable. CARA is either ignoring it, or cannot tell.

C: You know what's funny? The woman, who interviewed me, at the station, after it happened, was the same one who I ran away from at my house, when Ben got nicked. I mean, what are the chances, like, it being the same one. The same woman—and, yeah. I thought she'd be really angry at me, Like I saw her and thought, oh fuck, like is it all going to go to shit now? Cos, you know if she was, like, annoyed at me, for running away, then we'd be, well I dunno, it would all be a bit fucked, so I was worried. But it ended up being fine. More than fine, actually. She said she was happy to see me. Isn't that a weird thing to say? Like I'm giving a statement cos this girl has just died, and she said she was happy to see me. She said she wished it was "under better circumstances". I was just nodding, like yeah, obviously it's a bit shit, but then she said she knew I'd been through a lot, with everything, and then she held my hand, for a little but, before the interview started. She said if I wanted to stop at any point, then I should just say so. But I didn't have to. I never had to. And she just kept smiling and nodding and looking all sad at—me—I suppose? Just looking at me. Us two, on the table.

K: What about your chaperone?

C: He was fucking useless. Said fuck all. Did fuck all. Some social worker—wanker.

K: Oh... right.

C: Who did you have?

K: My Aunt.

C: I thought she didn't do that sort of law.

KELLY shrugs.

K: Mum thought it'd be useful. She was too emotional to be in the room. Kept going "what if it was you?" But it couldn't have been me, could it? Cos I can fucking swim.

C: Right. Well. I think I'm gonna start netball again.

K: Really?

C: Yeah. If you're gonna be the captain now.

K: Oh. Right.

C: You know they're having a vigil. For her. Tonight.

K: Yeah. I heard.

C: Are you gonna go?

K: Mum's making me. Says it's the right thing to do.

C: Yeah.

K: Are you?

C: Dunno. Maybe. Don't really like the idea of being around all those people talking about death, you know? It's a bit... yeah, grim, I dunno.

K: Yeah. Well, no... No, actually I don't. I don't get it. Cos like... why do you get to ignore it? Why do you get to pretend it didn't happen? That we weren't—you know—that we didn't—

C: That we didn't—what?

K: This plan, Cara. Your plan.

C: *Our* plan.

K: What the fuck? What the fuck did we do?

C: We did what we had to.

K: It was wrong. It was too far. What we did.

C: It was a fucking accident, Kelly. Shit happens, that's life. You get over it. You've got to. I do it all the time. No one ever fucking cares.

K: Oh fuck off.

C: Nah. You. You fuck off. Cos this is it. Like, people are noticing me now.

K: We're on the news.

C: She's on the news. We aren't. Not by name anyways. Child One and Child Two.

K: Jesus Christ, you're so / fucking—

C: I've got people that never even spat my way before coming up to me in Tesco's, telling me that they're so sorry about what happened to me, that I'm nothing like my wrong-un brother, or like my Mum. That I'm better than both of them, that I'm the sort of person that cares, the sort of person that would risk their life to go back for someone.

They're saying I'm kind, that I'm brave, that I'm strong, I'm really strong, and I do feel it, you know, I do feel strong. And if it was wrong, if it was so fucking wrong, then why hasn't anything happened?

K: There's an investigation. There's gonna be more questions. More people, more police. Don't think that it's gonna go away.

C: They won't find anything. I burnt her phone.

K: You what?

C: You could say thank you? I did it for you.

K: This is fucked.

C: You're so paranoid. Stop acting fucking traumatised.

K: This is so fucking fucked.

C: Whatever. I'm gonna go. See you Monday, yeah?

K: Yeah... no. No, I won't be in on Monday.

C: Fucking hell. How long are you gonna skive off for?

K: I'm not skiving. I'm... I'm going to a new school.

C: What?

K: Yeah.

A beat.

CARA looks pained.

C: Why would you want to do that?

K: My Mum said / it would—

C: Oh my God, every time, every fucking time, it's about your Mum. Haven't you got a fucking brain of your own?

K: Oh fuck off. Fuck you, Cara.

C: What school is it then?

K: What, are you gonna turn up at the gates?

C: What one is it?

A beat.

K: It's Kings.

C: What—the private school? Are you that desperate to get away from me?

K: I am. Actually. Is that what you want me to say? Look at the shit being around you has got me into. I didn't want this, I didn't want any of this. I just wanted things to stay the same. I just wanted everything to stay the same, how it used to be. I was happy—or at least I thought I was. Cos why wouldn't I be? And now—now my Mum can't even look me in the fucking eye. You know, I think she knows? She'd never say it. But she keeps saying I can tell her anything, that I don't have to hide anything from her. I can feel it. And she says I shouldn't go to the concert. That I should take some time for myself. She sold the tickets so I could go on a fucking trauma bootcamp with her. And now, now I have to leave behind all of my friends, all of our lot, because of you. Gonna have to be a nobody, being that girl, that weird girl that joins mid-way through term. Mid-way through the fucking year. Fuck being captain of the netball team. I'll have to start again, start again with everything. And everyone's gonna know. Everyone's gonna know that it's because of what happened. And you can say it's a random accident, but people aren't fucking stupid. Who's gonna want to be mates with me when I'm cursed? So yeah, it is because of you, you and all your fucking problems, cos you blame everyone else for all your shit, you and your junkie Mum and your twisted brother, and your 'Dad' who doesn't give a fuck, you blame everyone else, the entire

68

fucking world, for your fucked up life. And you told me, you fucking told me, "this isn't us", well it is. It is us. This, this whole—all of this. And it's not gone away. None of it. It's just so, so much worse.

KELLY begins to cry.

CARA tries to comfort her, but KELLY pushes her away, roughly.

K: You'll get what's coming to you.

C: So will you.

KELLY storms off stage, CARA shouts after her.

C: You're the one who pulled her in. Not me. Not. Me.

CARA is left alone on stage. She tuts, and sighs to herself.

She looks up, feels the audience around her, feels judged. She glares out, defiant.

Lights down.

XII.

EPILOGUE.

Several years later. The girls, now young women, are 22 years old. Bus stop.

KELLY is sat, listening to music, scrolling on her phone.

CARA enters, does a double take, and taps KELLY on the shoulder. KELLY, hardly looks up at CARA.

C: Oi. Oi!

K: Sorry, really sorry, I haven't / got any—

C: Kelly!

KELLY looks at CARA properly.

C: I thought it was you! You waiting?

K: Oh. Yeah, yes. I suppose I am.

CARA gets out a cigarette.

C: Do you mind?

K: No, no, please. Go ahead.

CARA lights her cigarette and begins to smoke.

C: Nice outfit.

K: Oh. Thanks.

KELLY laughs awkwardly.

K: It's so... formal. I have to wear it. For my grad scheme?

C: ...

K: It's like a, job, thing, you do, after you graduate.

C: Oh yeah. Right. I heard you went to Oxford or something.

K: Cambridge.

CARA shrugs.

C: What you listening to then?

K: Oh it was... it was stupid. Taylor Swift. Shit stuff.

C: Oh yeah. You always liked her.

K: Yeah, I did, back then.

The two speak at the same time.

C: How come you're back here, then?

K: How's your family, then?

The two stop speaking abruptly.

K: Oh—sorry.

C: No, no, it's fine. Family's good. Mum's alright, she's been clean for a couple of years now. Ben, my brother, you remember Ben? He's in Ibiza, or something. Lives out there now. Promoting for DJs and stuff. Looks decent, to be fair, might join him. Bit harder now, cos of visas and stuff, but yeah. Hoping to go out and join him. Dad's still Dad. Same old. Actually divorced Mum in the end, not that I ever thought he'd get round to it. Well, he had to, eventually. Cos of his new family. His new wife, whatever.

K: Oh that's good. That's really nice to hear, actually. Not the divorce... and the family, obviously. The other stuff. I always did hope your Mum would, you know, eventually— yeah. So that's really good.

C: Thanks.

K: So you're planning on leaving soon, then, to Spain?

C: Yeah. Eventually. Hard though. When you put down roots. Sometimes it feels like they've wrapped themselves around your wrists. Pulling you down when you try and leave. Don't suppose you ever felt like that though? Surprised to see you back. Hardly ever see you around town, even in the holidays.

K: Well, I just came down to see my Mum. She got quite poorly, earlier this year. So I'm just trying to see her more. She should be on the mend soon. We hope. Just waiting for the all clear now, but it's torture. You know how it is.

C: Oh yeah. Good that she's getting better. You know, I see her, sometimes. Out and about. Your Mum. Never says hi to me though.

K: Yeah, she was always a bit of a funny one, when it came to my friends.

C: To me, you mean.

CARA stubs out her cigarette.

K: What are you up to now, then?

C: Oh, you know how it is. Still in the same flat. Work for the new owners downstairs, sometimes, at the chippy.

K: They always did the best fish and chips.

C: Especially when they were free.

K: Yeah, or when you'd nick them when the guy at the till wasn't looking.

C: Only the chips! Nothing that'd hurt the business, you know, cheap as chips. I wasn't that bad as a kid.

K: Yeah... yeah, I suppose not.

C: Neither were you. And I knew you best.

K: Yeah, you did.

C: And you knew me. Thick as thieves, us two. Would've done anything for you. Back then.

A beat.

C: D'you ever think about it? About us? About her?

A beat.

KELLY leans out and waves for the bus.

K: Well. This is me.

C: It was good to see you. Let me know how long you're about for. Might be nice to actually, like, catch up.

K: Yeah, yeah, I'll... I'll let you know. Still got the same number?

C: Yeah. I do.

K: Cool. Yeah. Cool.

The two women stare at each other, neither saying anything.

C: You gonna get on your bus then?

KELLY moves to leave. As she does so, she turns around, stops. The two women face each other. Time seems to stand still.

Slowly, but decidedly, they begin to remove their clothes. They are in their underwear. It is childlike, vest tops and pattered underpants.

'I Love It' begins playing. The two women, girls now, begin to dance, and scream the lyrics. Lights down.

END.

ALSO AVAILABLE FROM SALAMANDER STREET

A PLAY, A PIE AND A PINT: VOLUME TWO
8 One-Act Plays from Òran Mór.
ISBN: 9781068696237

To celebrate the beloved Glasow theatrical institution's 20th anniversary, this second collection includes critically acclaimed plays and favourites as voted by the public and members of the theatre company.

PLACEHOLDER by Catherine Bisset
ISBN: 9781068696282

A parallel text version of Catherine Bisset's dramatic solo play set in 1790 Saint-Domingue – the daughter of an enslaved woman reflects on her life as an opera singer and the importance of resistance.

COWBOYS AND LESBIANS
by Billie Esplen
ISBN: 9781914228902

When repressed British schoolfriends Nina and Noa start writing a parody American coming-of-age romance, the colourful, familiar characters come to life and show them that they might just have a story of their own to tell.

GROUP PORTRAIT IN A SUMMER LANDSCAPE
by Peter Arnott
ISBN: 9781914228933

An intense and riveting play set in a Perthshire country house during the Scottish Independence referendum of 2014. A retired academic and political heavyweight invites family and former students together for a dramatic reckoning.

www.ingramcontent.com/pod-product-compliance
Lightning Source LLC
Chambersburg PA
CBHW052206090426
42741CB00010B/2427